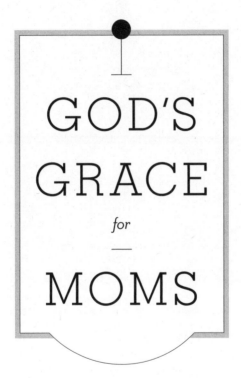

GOD'S GRACE

GRACE

for

MOMS

B&H
PUBLISHING GROUP

NASHVILLE, TENNESSEE

978-1-5359-1752-0

Published by B&H Publishing Group
Nashville, Tennessee

Dewey Decimal Classification: 234.1
Subject Heading: GRACE (THEOLOGY) / HOPE / SELF-CONFIDENCE

1 2 3 4 5 6 7 8 · 22 21 20 19 18

CONTENTS

INTRODUCTION

Life tends to maneuver us into categories, into penciled-in bubbles on the random identification form. Some of them we like; some we don't. Some we actively seek out and continue to pursue; some are sitting there waiting for us and won't turn us loose.

But one thing we all know: deep inside these simple boxes and check marks reside entire worlds crawling with complication, challenge, and difficulty. Even if easy to get into, they are rarely so easy to faithfully, successfully, and steadily keep going through.

As a mom, for instance, you may often feel inadequate to the tasks thrust upon you or ahead of you. Your days are likely full of activity yet can still feel unfinished. No matter how old your children are, your job will never really be finished. You try maximizing the jobs your particular boxes entail; yet they maddeningly resist being colored all the way to the edges.

The reason this book exists is because God's grace never met a check box it couldn't fill with hope, peace, direction, and perspective—with motivation, counsel, freedom, and opportunity. This book is here, and is now yours, because the Bible not only speaks timelessly to everyone but specifically to you . . . with grace. God's grace. Sufficient to every place. Even to the places you're living this very moment.

ACCEPTANCE

When we are faced with family conflicts, job stresses, or uncertainty about the future, we can rest in knowing that God's love for us is constant.

∽

But the LORD said to Samuel, "Do not look at his appearance or his stature because I have rejected him. Humans do not see what the LORD sees, for humans see what is visible, but the LORD sees the heart."
    1 Samuel 16:7

∽

"Everyone the Father gives me will come to me, and the one who comes to me I will never cast out."
    John 6:37

∽

But God proves his own love for us in that while we were still sinners, Christ died for us.
    Romans 5:8

If God is for us, who is against us?
    Romans 8:31

❧

Peter began to speak: "Now I truly understand that God doesn't show favoritism, but in every nation the person who fears him and does what is right is acceptable to him."
    Acts 10:34–35

❧

Heavenly Father, thank You that no matter what trials and stressors I might face, You uphold me and guide me according to Your purposes.

ANGER

Anger is an emotion that can reveal to us our values. The key, however, is not to act out in anger but to speak and act with love.

❧

Refrain from anger and give up your rage;
do not be agitated—it can only bring harm.
    Psalm 37:8

❧

A patient person shows great understanding,
but a quick-tempered one promotes foolishness.
    Proverbs 14:29

❧

A gentle answer turns away anger,
but a harsh word stirs up wrath.
    Proverbs 15:1

"But I tell you, everyone who is angry with his brother or sister will be subject to judgment. Whoever insults his brother or sister, will be subject to the court. Whoever says, 'You fool!' will be subject to hellfire."
Matthew 5:22

❧

Be angry and do not sin. Don't let the sun go down on your anger, and don't give the devil an opportunity.
Ephesians 4:26–27

❧

Lord, may Your Holy Spirit guide my words and actions when I'm feeling angry so that I can show grace to my spouse, children, and others around me.

ANXIETY

Beneath our anxieties is a need to feel in control—but our peace is found in knowing that the Creator of the universe holds us safely in the palm of His hand.

✑

"Therefore I tell you: Don't worry about your life, what you will eat or what you will drink; or about your body, what you will wear. Isn't life more than food and the body more than clothing? Consider the birds of the sky: They don't sow or reap or gather into barns, yet your heavenly Father feeds them. Aren't you worth more than they? Can any of you add one moment to his life-span by worrying?"
  Matthew 6:25–27

✑

"Peace I leave with you. My peace I give to you. I do not give to you as the world gives. Don't let your heart be troubled or fearful."
  John 14:27

Don't worry about anything, but in everything, through prayer and petition with thanksgiving, present your requests to God. And the peace of God, which surpasses all understanding, will guard your hearts and minds in Christ Jesus.

Philippians 4:6–7

❧

For God has not given us a spirit of fear, but one of power, love, and sound judgment.

2 Timothy 1:7

❧

Humble yourselves, therefore, under the mighty hand of God, so that he may exalt you at the proper time, casting all your cares on him, because he cares about you.

1 Peter 5:6–7

❧

Heavenly Father, I entrust to You my family, my children, our finances, and my well-being, knowing that Your peace will guard my heart and mind.

AUTHORITY

As a mom, you hold a particular position of authority over your children, and as such, you have the opportunity to reveal to them the very character of God.

∾

Then he said to them, "Give, then, to Caesar the things that are Caesar's, and to God the things that are God's." When they heard this, they were amazed. So they left him and went away.
Matthew 22:21–22

∾

Jesus came near and said to them, "All authority has been given to me in heaven and on earth."
Matthew 28:18

∾

Let everyone submit to the governing authorities, since there is no authority except from God, and the authorities that exist are instituted by God.
Romans 13:1

For this reason God highly exalted him
and gave him the name
that is above every name,
so that at the name of Jesus
every knee will bow—
in heaven and on earth
and under the earth—
and every tongue will confess
that Jesus Christ is Lord,
to the glory of God the Father.
  Philippians 2:9–11

∽

Submit to every human authority because of the Lord, whether to the
emperor as the supreme authority or to governors as those sent out
by him to punish those who do what is evil and to praise those who do
what is good. For it is God's will that you silence the ignorance of foolish
people by doing good.
  1 Peter 2:13–15

∽

Father God, please grant me wisdom and grace to
be a mirror of godly authority in my family, and I
willingly submit to Your authority in all situations.

BEAUTY

All of creation is ablaze with the beauty of the Lord—
look for it in sunsets, the night stars, blooms of flowers,
and the glowing face of your children.

∽

I have asked one thing from the LORD;
it is what I desire:
to dwell in the house of the LORD
all the days of my life,
gazing on the beauty of the LORD
and seeking him in his temple.
    Psalm 27:4

∽

I will praise you
because I have been remarkably and wondrously made.
Your works are wondrous,
and I know this very well.
    Psalm 139:14

Charm is deceptive and beauty is fleeting,
but a woman who fears the LORD will be praised.
    Proverbs 31:30

◈

You are absolutely beautiful, my darling;
there is no imperfection in you.
    Song of Solomon 4:7

◈

*Don't let your beauty consist of outward things like elaborate hairstyles
and wearing gold jewelry, but rather what is inside the heart—the
imperishable quality of a gentle and quiet spirit, which is of great worth
in God's sight.*
    1 Peter 3:3–4

◈

*Heavenly Father, I thank You and praise You for the
beauty You have poured out on this earth, which
heals and blesses the hearts that behold it.*

BLESSINGS

We can experience deep joy when we take notice of the abundant blessings in our lives and praise and thank the Lord for such bountiful grace.

❧

"May the LORD bless you and protect you; may the LORD make his face shine on you and be gracious to you; may the LORD look with favor on you and give you peace."
    Numbers 6:24–26

❧

Indeed, we have all received grace upon grace from his fullness, for the law was given through Moses; grace and truth came through Jesus Christ.
    John 1:16–17

And God is able to make every grace overflow to you, so that in every way, always having everything you need, you may excel in every good work.
    2 Corinthians 9:8

༺

Blessed is the God and Father of our Lord Jesus Christ, who has blessed us with every spiritual blessing in the heavens in Christ.
    Ephesians 1:3

༺

And my God will supply all your needs according to his riches in glory in Christ Jesus.
    Philippians 4:19

༺

Heavenly Father, I thank You and praise You for all the ways You have shown me mercy and grace, and I ask for the blessing of Your presence throughout this day.

CARING

Moms play an essential role in their children's lives: you reflect the character of God as a tender parent, a nurturer, and a comforter during hard times.

❧

"I give you a new command: Love one another. Just as I have loved you, you are also to love one another. By this everyone will know that you are my disciples, if you love one another."
  John 13:34–35

❧

Carry one another's burdens; in this way you will fulfill the law of Christ.
  Galatians 6:2

Therefore, as we have opportunity, let us work for the good of all,
especially for those who belong to the household of faith.
    Galatians 6:10

∽

Everyone should look out not only for his own interests, but also for the
interests of others.
    Philippians 2:4

∽

Heavenly Father, help me reflect Your gracious
patience and unfailing love to my children.

CHILDREN

Children are a heritage from the Lord and a precious gift to be stewarded with love, mercy, and grace.

⁐

Sons are indeed a heritage from the LORD,
offspring, a reward.
Like arrows in the hand of a warrior
are the sons born in one's youth.
Happy is the man who has filled his quiver with them.
They will never be put to shame
when they speak with their enemies at the city gate.
*   Psalm 127:3–5*

⁐

Even a young man is known by his actions—
by whether his behavior is pure and upright.
*   Proverbs 20:11*

When Jesus saw it, he was indignant and said to them, "Let the little children come to me. Don't stop them, because the kingdom of God belongs to such as these."
    Mark 10:14

∾

Fathers, don't stir up anger in your children, but bring them up in the training and instruction of the Lord.
    Ephesians 6:4

∾

Children, obey your parents in everything, for this pleases the Lord.
    Colossians 3:20

∾

Dear Jesus, may my children be a reminder that Your kingdom belongs to those with a childlike heart and mind.

COMFORT

None of us are immune from hardships, loss, and grief, but we can take heart that no matter what has happened, the Lord promises to comfort us.

❧

Even when I go through the darkest valley,
I fear no danger,
for you are with me;
your rod and your staff—they comfort me.
    Psalm 23:4

❧

Remember your word to your servant;
you have given me hope through it.
This is my comfort in my affliction:
Your promise has given me life.
    Psalm 119:49–50

As a mother comforts her son, so I will comfort you, and you will be comforted in Jerusalem.
    Isaiah 66:13

༄

"Blessed are those who mourn, for they will be comforted."
    Matthew 5:4

༄

Blessed be the God and Father of our Lord Jesus Christ, the Father of mercies and the God of all comfort. He comforts us in all our affliction, so that we may be able to comfort those who are in any kind of affliction, through the comfort we ourselves receive from God.
    2 Corinthians 1:3–4

༄

*Dear God, thank You for comforting me
and healing my heart in times of trial,
and may I be a source of comfort for others.*

COMPASSION

The Lord commands us to love our neighbors as ourselves and to also love our enemies—godly compassion is speaking and acting out of love in the best interest of others.

❧

Yet he was compassionate;
he atoned for their iniquity
and did not destroy them.
He often turned his anger aside
and did not unleash all his wrath.
    Psalm 78:38

❧

When he went ashore, he saw a large crowd and had compassion on them, because they were like sheep without a shepherd. Then he began to teach them many things.
    Mark 6:34

Carry one another's burdens; in this way you will fulfill the law of Christ.
   Galatians 6:2

⁓

And be kind and compassionate to one another, forgiving one another, just as God also forgave you in Christ.
   Ephesians 4:32

⁓

Lord, may Your Holy Spirit fill my heart and soul with concern for my family, neighbors, and colleagues so that I may be a willing conduit of Your love.

CONFLICT

One way we can walk in the Spirit, rather than according to the flesh, is to resist the pride and need to be right that we often feel in conflicts with others.

∽

"If your brother sins against you, go and rebuke him in private. If he listens to you, you have won your brother. But if he won't listen, take one or two others with you, so that by the testimony of two or three witnesses every fact may be established. If he doesn't pay attention to them, tell the church. If he doesn't pay attention even to the church, let him be like a Gentile and a tax collector to you."
    Matthew 18:15–17

∽

Bless those who persecute you; bless and do not curse. Rejoice with those who rejoice; weep with those who weep. Live in harmony with one another. Do not be proud; instead, associate with the humble. Do not be wise in your own estimation. Do not repay anyone evil for evil. Give careful thought to do what is honorable in everyone's eyes. If possible, as far as it depends on you, live at peace with everyone.
    Romans 12:14–18

A gentle answer turns away anger,
but a harsh word stirs up wrath.
Proverbs 15:1

599

Therefore, putting away lying, speak the truth, each one to his neighbor,
because we are members of one another. Be angry and do not sin. Don't let
the sun go down on your anger, and don't give the devil an opportunity.
Ephesians 4:25–27

599

What is the source of wars and fights among you? Don't they come from
your passions that wage war within you? You desire and do not have.
You murder and covet and cannot obtain. You fight and wage war. You
do not have because you do not ask.
James 4:1–2

599

Lord Jesus, may I imitate Your grace and
gentleness in any disagreement or
confrontation with other people in my life.

CONTENTMENT

The quickest route to contentment is through gratitude and trust—recognize the abundant goodness in your life and trust that God never fails to provide for your needs.

∽

"So don't worry, saying, 'What will we eat?' or 'What will we drink?' or 'What will we wear?' For the Gentiles eagerly seek all these things, and your heavenly Father knows that you need them. But seek first the kingdom of God and his righteousness, and all these things will be provided for you. Therefore don't worry about tomorrow, because tomorrow will worry about itself. Each day has enough trouble of its own."
    Matthew 6:31–34

∽

He then told them, "Watch out and be on guard against all greed, because one's life is not in the abundance of his possessions."
    Luke 12:15

I don't say this out of need, for I have learned to be content in whatever circumstances I find myself. I know both how to make do with little, and I know how to make do with a lot. In any and all circumstances I have learned the secret of being content—whether well fed or hungry, whether in abundance or in need.

Philippians 4:11–12

✍

But godliness with contentment is great gain. For we brought nothing into the world, and we can take nothing out. If we have food and clothing, we will be content with these.

1 Timothy 6:6–8

✍

Keep your life free from the love of money. Be satisfied with what you have, for he himself has said, I will never leave you or abandon you.

Hebrews 13:5

✍

Heavenly Father, thank You for your unfailing love and faithfulness, and may You grow in me a godly contentment.

COURAGE

Having courage doesn't mean that you feel no fear; rather it means having a willingness and readiness to proceed despite the fear.

✍

"Haven't I commanded you: be strong and courageous? Do not be afraid or discouraged, for the LORD your God is with you wherever you go."
>   *Joshua 1:9*

✍

I always let the LORD guide me.
Because he is at my right hand,
I will not be shaken.
>   *Psalm 16:8*

Wait for the LORD;
be strong, and let your heart be courageous.
Wait for the LORD.
    Psalm 27:14

⁇

Be alert, stand firm in the faith, be courageous, be strong.
    1 Corinthians 16:13

⁇

For God has not given us a spirit of fear, but one of power, love, and
sound judgment.
    2 Timothy 1:7

⁇

Dear God, grant me a sense of Your
strength and presence that I may face
this day and its challenges with courage.

COVENANT

God's covenant with us through the blood of Jesus assures us that we are His people, forgiven and deeply loved.

∽

He remembers his covenant forever,
the promise he ordained
for a thousand generations—
the covenant he made with Abraham,
swore to Isaac,
and confirmed to Jacob as a decree
and to Israel as a permanent covenant:
"I will give the land of Canaan to you
as your inherited portion."
    Psalm 105:8–11

∽

"For this is my blood of the covenant, which is poured out for many for the forgiveness of sins."
    Matthew 26:28

"Look, the days are coming"—this is the LORD's declaration—"when I
will make a new covenant with the house of Israel and with the house of
Judah. This one will not be like the covenant I made with their ancestors
on the day I took them by the hand to lead them out of the land of
Egypt—my covenant that they broke even though I am their master"—
the LORD's declaration. "Instead, this is the covenant I will make with
the house of Israel after those days"—the LORD's declaration. "I will put
my teaching within them and write it on their hearts. I will be their God,
and they will be my people. No longer will one teach his neighbor or his
brother, saying, 'Know the LORD,' for they will all know me, from the
least to the greatest of them"—this is the LORD's declaration. "For I will
forgive their iniquity and never again remember their sin."
    Jeremiah 31:31–34

⁓

Therefore, he is the mediator of a new covenant, so that those who are
called might receive the promise of the eternal inheritance, because
a death has taken place for redemption from the transgressions
committed under the first covenant.
    Hebrews 9:15

⁓

*Heavenly Father, may Your Holy Spirit
impress upon my heart Your Word and Your
ways that I may glorify You in all I do and say.*

DEPRESSION

When your heart is heavy and your mind is burdened, hold fast to the truth that God comforts us in all of our afflictions so that we may be able to comfort others with His love.

∽

The LORD is near the brokenhearted;
he saves those crushed in spirit.
        Psalm 34:18

∽

Answer me quickly, LORD;
my spirit fails.
Don't hide your face from me,
or I will be like those
going down to the Pit.
Let me experience
your faithful love in the morning,
for I trust in you.
Reveal to me the way I should go
because I appeal to you.
        Psalm 143:7–8

The LORD sits enthroned over the flood;
the LORD sits enthroned, King forever.
The LORD gives his people strength;
the LORD blesses his people with peace.
   Psalm 29:10–11

∽

"Do not fear, for I am with you; do not be afraid, for I am your God.
I will strengthen you; I will help you; I will hold on to you with my
righteous right hand."
   Isaiah 41:10

∽

"I will give you the treasures of darkness and riches from secret places,
so that you may know that I am the LORD. I am the God of Israel, who
calls you by your name."
   Isaiah 45:3

∽

Dear Jesus, You were a man of sorrows
and acquainted with grief—please fill
my heart with Your strength and peace.

DISCERNMENT

The Holy Spirit is our ever-present Helper who grants us wisdom so that we can know and do the will of God.

✺

So give your servant a receptive heart to judge your people and to discern between good and evil. For who is able to judge this great people of yours?
    1 Kings 3:9

✺

And I pray this: that your love will keep on growing in knowledge and every kind of discernment, so that you may approve the things that are superior and may be pure and blameless in the day of Christ.
    Philippians 1:9–10

✺

Don't stifle the Spirit. Don't despise prophecies, but test all things. Hold on to what is good. Stay away from every kind of evil.
    1 Thessalonians 5:19-22

Now if any of you lacks wisdom, he should ask God—who gives to all generously and ungrudgingly—and it will be given to him.
    James 1:5

❧

Dear friends, do not believe every spirit, but test the spirits to see if they are from God, because many false prophets have gone out into the world.
    1 John 4:1

❧

Holy Spirit, may my spirit be open and receptive to Your prompting and leading so that I discern what is right and good in all things.

DISCIPLINE

As a mom, you're faced with enforcing rules on a daily basis—let the tender heart of God be your guide as you instill discipline in your children.

෨

Whoever loves discipline loves knowledge,
but one who hates correction is stupid.
 Proverbs 12:1

෨

The one who will not use the rod hates his son,
but the one who loves him disciplines him diligently.
 Proverbs 13:24

෨

Foolishness is bound to the heart of a youth;
a rod of discipline will separate it from him.
 Proverbs 22:15

Instead, I discipline my body and bring it under strict control, so that after preaching to others, I myself will not be disqualified.
     1 Corinthians 9:27

∽

No discipline seems enjoyable at the time, but painful. Later on, however, it yields the peaceful fruit of righteousness to those who have been trained by it.
     Hebrews 12:11

∽

Heavenly Father, may Your hand guide me and correct me so that all I do and say will glorify You.

DISSATISFIED

When we feel dissatisfied with our lives or circumstances, we can rediscover the abundance around us by practicing gratitude and thanksgiving.

❧

For he has satisfied the thirsty
and filled the hungry with good things.
    Psalm 107:9

❧

You open your hand
and satisfy the desire of every living thing.
    Psalm 145:16

❧

The LORD will always lead you, satisfy you in a parched land, and
strengthen your bones. You will be like a watered garden and like a
spring whose water never runs dry.
    Isaiah 58:11

"I am the bread of life," Jesus told them. "No one who comes to me will ever be hungry, and no one who believes in me will ever be thirsty again."
John 6:35

✑

Now may the God of hope fill you with all joy and peace as you believe so that you may overflow with hope by the power of the Holy Spirit.
Romans 15:13

✑

Dear God, no good thing do You withhold from Your people. Help me see the goodness all around me and delight in Your good and perfect gifts.

ENCOURAGEMENT

We can experience deep gladness from knowing that our God goes before us and is with us at all times.

❧

The LORD is the one who will go before you. He will be with you; he will not leave you or abandon you. Do not be afraid or discouraged.
Deuteronomy 31:8

❧

God is our refuge and strength,
a helper who is always found
in times of trouble.
Psalm 46:1

❧

"Aren't five sparrows sold for two pennies? Yet not one of them is forgotten in God's sight. Indeed, the hairs of your head are all counted. Don't be afraid; you are worth more than many sparrows."
Luke 12:6–7

"I have told you these things so that in me you may have peace. You will have suffering in this world. Be courageous! I have conquered the world."

    John 16:33

℘

And let us watch out for one another to provoke love and good works, not neglecting to gather together, as some are in the habit of doing, but encouraging each other, and all the more as you see the day approaching.

    Hebrews 10:24–25

℘

*Christ Jesus, may Your Spirit strengthen
and encourage my heart today, that I may
be a source of encouragement for those
I encounter throughout the day.*

FAILURE

Though failures of any kind can crush our spirits, we have the assurance that God's purposes can never be thwarted.

❦

A person's steps are established by the LORD,
and he takes pleasure in his way.
Though he falls, he will not be overwhelmed,
because the LORD supports him with his hand.
　　Psalm 37:23–24

❦

He brought me up from a desolate pit,
out of the muddy clay,
and set my feet on a rock,
making my steps secure.
He put a new song in my mouth,
a hymn of praise to our God.
Many will see and fear,
and they will trust in the LORD.
　　Psalm 40:2–3

And not only that, but we also rejoice in our afflictions, because we know that affliction produces endurance, endurance produces proven character, and proven character produces hope.

Romans 5:3–4

∽

Now we have this treasure in clay jars, so that this extraordinary power may be from God and not from us. We are afflicted in every way but not crushed; we are perplexed but not in despair; we are persecuted but not abandoned; we are struck down but not destroyed.

2 Corinthians 4:7–9

∽

Brothers and sisters, I do not consider myself to have taken hold of it. But one thing I do: Forgetting what is behind and reaching forward to what is ahead, I pursue as my goal the prize promised by God's heavenly call in Christ Jesus.

Philippians 3:13–14

∽

Heavenly Father, grant me grace in times of failure and help me press forward as I fix my eyes on Jesus.

FAITHFULNESS

God's everlasting faithfulness to His people is a deep source of hope, as well as an inspiration for how we should conduct ourselves in our relationships.

✍

Because of the LORD's faithful love
we do not perish,
for his mercies never end.
They are new every morning;
great is your faithfulness!
      Lamentations 3:22–23

✍

"His master said to him, 'Well done, good and faithful servant! You were faithful over a few things; I will put you in charge of many things. Share your master's joy.'"
      Matthew 25:21

"Whoever is faithful in very little is also faithful in much, and whoever is unrighteous in very little is also unrighteous in much. So if you have not been faithful with worldly wealth, who will trust you with what is genuine? And if you have not been faithful with what belongs to someone else, who will give you what is your own?"
　Luke 16:10–12

∽

If we are faithless, he remains faithful, for he cannot deny himself.
　2 Timothy 2:13

∽

Let us hold on to the confession of our hope without wavering, since he who promised is faithful.
　Hebrews 10:23

∽

Dear God, whose mercies are new every morning, grant me wisdom to be faithful to my family, my church, and my community.

FAMILY

Mothers have a special calling to encourage, nurture, and teach their children so they grow up with the knowledge and experience of God's love.

❧

This is why a man leaves his father and mother and bonds with his wife, and they become one flesh.

      Genesis 2:24

❧

Wives, submit to your husbands as to the Lord, because the husband is the head of the wife as Christ is the head of the church. He is the Savior of the body. Now as the church submits to Christ, so also wives are to submit to their husbands in everything. Husbands, love your wives, just as Christ loved the church and gave himself for her to make her holy, cleansing her with the washing of water by the word. He did this to present the church to himself in splendor, without spot or wrinkle or anything like that, but holy and blameless. In the same way, husbands are to love their wives as their own bodies. He who loves his wife loves himself.

      Ephesians 5:22–28

"Honor your father and your mother so that you may have a long life in the land that the LORD your God is giving you."

Exodus 20:12

ℰ∕∂

Sons are indeed a heritage from the LORD,
offspring, a reward.
Like arrows in the hand of a warrior
are the sons born in one's youth.
Happy is the man who has filled his quiver with them.
They will never be put to shame
when they speak with their enemies at the city gate.

Psalm 127:3–5

ℰ∕∂

Fathers, don't stir up anger in your children, but bring them up in the training and instruction of the Lord.

Ephesians 6:4

ℰ∕∂

Lord God, may I be a reflection of Your love and strength to my family in all I do and say.

FEAR

Most of our dread comes not from an immediate threat but from fear of what might happen—but this is false fear. We have an almighty God who loves us and cares for us at all times.

∽

"Haven't I commanded you: be strong and courageous? Do not be afraid or discouraged, for the LORD your God is with you wherever you go."
   Joshua 1:9

∽

When I am afraid,
I will trust in you.
   Psalm 56:3

∽

You did not receive a spirit of slavery to fall back into fear. Instead, you received the Spirit of adoption, by whom we cry out, "Abba, Father!"
   Romans 8:15

For God has not given us a spirit of fear, but one of power, love, and sound judgment.
    2 Timothy 1:7

✍

Humble yourselves, therefore, under the mighty hand of God, so that he may exalt you at the proper time, casting all your cares on him, because he cares about you.
    1 Peter 5:6–7

✍

Abba, Father, I cry out to You for Your protection and comfort in times when I'm afraid. Thank You for Your faithful love and comfort.

FELLOWSHIP

As a mom constantly busy with children, school, work, and family obligations, fellowship with other women and fellow believers can refresh your heart and soul.

✍

Iron sharpens iron,
and one person sharpens another.
> *Proverbs 27:17*

✍

Two are better than one because they have a good reward for their efforts. For if either falls, his companion can lift him up; but pity the one who falls without another to lift him up.
> *Ecclesiastes 4:9–10*

✍

Carry one another's burdens; in this way you will fulfill the law of Christ.
> *Galatians 6:2*

Therefore encourage one another and build each other up as you are already doing.
    1 Thessalonians 5:11

☙

And let us watch out for one another to provoke love and good works, not neglecting to gather together, as some are in the habit of doing, but encouraging each other, and all the more as you see the day approaching.
    Hebrews 10:24–25

☙

Dear Jesus, my heavenly Friend, please reveal to me ways I can spend more time in fellowship and build up others in my community.

FORGIVENESS

Forgiving someone who has hurt you means you no longer call to mind their fault or error—this extends grace to them and freedom for you.

∽

"Therefore I tell you, her many sins have been forgiven; that's why she loved much. But the one who is forgiven little, loves little."
     Luke 7:47

∽

Live in harmony with one another. Do not be proud; instead, associate with the humble. Do not be wise in your own estimation. Do not repay anyone evil for evil. Give careful thought to do what is honorable in everyone's eyes. If possible, as far as it depends on you, live at peace with everyone.
     Romans 12:16–18

Be kind and compassionate to one another, forgiving one another, just as God also forgave you in Christ.
Ephesians 4:32

♒

As God's chosen ones, holy and dearly loved, put on compassion, kindness, humility, gentleness, and patience, bearing with one another and forgiving one another if anyone has a grievance against another. Just as the Lord has forgiven you, so you are also to forgive.
Colossians 3:12–13

♒

Dear God, just as You forgave all my debts and wrongs through Christ, empower me to extend forgiveness to those who have mistreated or hurt me.

FRIENDSHIP

Precious are the friends, neighbors, and colleagues in our lives who faithfully stand by us through joys and sorrows, victories and failures, gains and loss.

∽

Iron sharpens iron,
and one person sharpens another.
> *Proverbs 27:17*

∽

Two are better than one because they have a good reward for their efforts. For if either falls, his companion can lift him up; but pity the one who falls without another to lift him up.
> *Ecclesiastes 4:9–10*

"No one has greater love than this: to lay down his life for his friends. You are my friends if you do what I command you. I do not call you servants anymore, because a servant doesn't know what his master is doing. I have called you friends, because I have made known to you everything I have heard from my Father."

John 15:13–15

∽

Dear friends, let us love one another, because love is from God, and everyone who loves has been born of God and knows God.

1 John 4:7

∽

Therefore encourage one another and build each other up as you are already doing.

1 Thessalonians 5:11

∽

Lord Jesus, who called His disciples friends, thank You for demonstrating God's love for us and how best to love one another.

FUTURE

God's grace and His purposes have assured your future, which grants you the freedom to live fully, faithfully, and courageously in the present moment.

∽

The LORD will fulfill his purpose for me.
LORD, your faithful love endures forever;
do not abandon the work of your hands.
        Psalm 138:8

∽

A person's heart plans his way,
but the LORD determines his steps.
        Proverbs 16:9

∽

"For I know the plans I have for you"—this is the LORD's declaration—
"plans for your well-being, not for disaster, to give you a future and a
hope."
        Jeremiah 29:11

But our citizenship is in heaven, and we eagerly wait for a Savior from there, the Lord Jesus Christ. He will transform the body of our humble condition into the likeness of his glorious body, by the power that enables him to subject everything to himself.

Philippians 3:20–21

∽

Dear friends, we are God's children now, and what we will be has not yet been revealed. We know that when he appears, we will be like him because we will see him as he is.

1 John 3:2

∽

Dear Lord, help me remember that my past, present, and future are all in Your hands.

GRACE

The greatest gift we will ever receive is grace—the wholly unmerited favor of the Most High.

✍

The law came along to multiply the trespass. But where sin multiplied, grace multiplied even more.
    Romans 5:20

✍

For sin will not rule over you, because you are not under the law but under grace.
    Romans 6:14

✍

Now if by grace, then it is not by works; otherwise grace ceases to be grace.
    Romans 11:6

But he said to me, "My grace is sufficient for you, for my power is perfected in weakness." Therefore, I will most gladly boast all the more about my weaknesses, so that Christ's power may reside in me.
    2 Corinthians 12:9

∽

For you are saved by grace through faith, and this is not from yourselves; it is God's gift—not from works, so that no one can boast.
    Ephesians 2:8–9

∽

Lord God, thank You for Your riches of grace that have been poured out on me through faith in Christ Jesus.

GRIEF

The deep sorrow of grief that comes from losing a loved one, a longtime friend, or even a pet can seem profound and unending—but God promises to be near us, to comfort us, and to bring joy and beauty out of the ashes.

∽

*The righteous cry out, and the L*ORD* hears,*
and rescues them from all their troubles.
*The L*ORD* is near the brokenhearted;*
he saves those crushed in spirit.
     Psalm 34:17–18

∽

Why, my soul, are you so dejected?
Why are you in such turmoil?
Put your hope in God, for I will still praise him,
my Savior and my God.
     Psalm 42:5

"Then the young women will rejoice with dancing,
while young and old men rejoice together.
I will turn their mourning into joy,
give them consolation,
and bring happiness out of grief."
    Jeremiah 31:13

∽

Though the fig tree does not bud and there is no fruit on the vines,
though the olive crop fails and the fields produce no food, though the
flocks disappear from the pen and there are no herds in the stalls, yet I
will celebrate in the LORD; I will rejoice in the God of my salvation!
    Habakkuk 3:17–18

∽

"So you also have sorrow now. But I will see you again. Your hearts will
rejoice, and no one will take away your joy from you."
    John 16:22

∽

Heavenly Father, when my heart is aching
and all I see is darkness, I trust that You
are my light and my salvation.

HAPPINESS

Though happiness sometimes comes from external circumstances, we experience the most lasting happiness by enjoying our union with Christ.

✑

Therefore my heart is glad
and my whole being rejoices;
my body also rests securely.
        Psalm 16:9

✑

Take delight in the LORD,
and he will give you your heart's desires.
        Psalm 37:4

A joyful heart makes a face cheerful,
but a sad heart produces a broken spirit.
    Proverbs 15:13

✐

I know that there is nothing better for them than to rejoice and enjoy the
good life.
    Ecclesiastes 3:12

✐

Rejoice in the Lord always. I will say it again: Rejoice!
    Philippians 4:4

✐

Lord Jesus, may my heart be happy
and cheerful because I know You.

HEALTH

Clean food and abundant exercise fortifies the heart and body, while time spent with God keeps our minds and spirits healthy.

✍

My flesh and my heart may fail,
but God is the strength of my heart,
my portion forever.
Psalm 73:26

✍

He heals the brokenhearted
and bandages their wounds.
Psalm 147:3

✍

So, whether you eat or drink, or whatever you do, do everything for the glory of God.
1 Corinthians 10:31

Don't be wise in your own eyes;
fear the Lord and turn away from evil.
This will be healing for your body
and strengthening for your bones.

> *Proverbs 3:7–8*

ↄ৶

Don't you know that your body is a temple of the Holy Spirit who is in you, whom you have from God? You are not your own, for you were bought at a price. So glorify God with your body.

> *1 Corinthians 6:19–20*

ↄ৶

Dear God, grant me wisdom for ways
to honor my body as the temple of the
Holy Spirit through my daily choices.

HOPE

It's tempting to put our hope in the wrong places—relationships, financial security, personal or professional abilities—but our firmest hope is found only in Christ Jesus.

∽

But those who trust in the LORD
will renew their strength;
they will soar on wings like eagles;
they will run and not become weary,
they will walk and not faint.
    Isaiah 40:31

∽

We have also obtained access through him by faith into this grace in which we stand, and we rejoice in the hope of the glory of God. And not only that, but we also rejoice in our afflictions, because we know that affliction produces endurance, endurance produces proven character, and proven character produces hope.
    Romans 5:2–4

I wait for the LORD; I wait
and put my hope in his word.
    Psalm 130:5

ༀ

Now may the God of hope fill you with all joy and peace as you believe
so that you may overflow with hope by the power of the Holy Spirit.
    Romans 15:13

ༀ

Let us run with endurance the race that lies before us, keeping our eyes
on Jesus, the source and perfecter of our faith. For the joy that lay before
him, he endured the cross, despising the shame, and sat down at the
right hand of the throne of God. For consider him who endured such
hostility from sinners against himself, so that you won't grow weary and
give up.
    Hebrews 12:1–3

ༀ

Lord of hope, please fill me with all
joy and peace as I hope in you.

HUMILITY

The key to cultivating true humility isn't to act self-deprecating but to simply not think of oneself much at all.

❧

Sitting down, he called the Twelve and said to them, "If anyone wants to be first, he must be last and servant of all."
   Mark 9:35

❧

Live in harmony with one another. Do not be proud; instead, associate with the humble. Do not be wise in your own estimation.
   Romans 12:16

❧

Do nothing out of selfish ambition or conceit, but in humility consider others as more important than yourselves.
   Philippians 2:3

Adopt the same attitude as that of Christ Jesus, who, existing in the form of God, did not consider equality with God as something to be exploited. Instead he emptied himself by assuming the form of a servant, taking on the likeness of humanity. And when he had come as a man, he humbled himself by becoming obedient to the point of death—even to death on a cross.

    Philippians 2:5–8

❧

Who among you is wise and understanding? By his good conduct he should show that his works are done in the gentleness that comes from wisdom.

    James 3:13

❧

Lord Jesus, who demonstrated perfect selflessness, please be my vision and my constant focus so that I forget myself completely.

INTEGRITY

The late basketball coach John Wooden once said, "The true test of a person's character is what he does when no one is watching."

⁂

The one who lives with integrity lives securely,
but whoever perverts his ways will be found out.
    Proverbs 10:9

⁂

Better the poor person who lives with integrity
than the rich one who distorts right and wrong.
    Proverbs 28:6

⁂

Indeed, we are giving careful thought to do what is right, not only before
the Lord but also before people.
    2 Corinthians 8:21

Whatever you do, do it from the heart, as something done for the Lord and not for people, knowing that you will receive the reward of an inheritance from the Lord. You serve the Lord Christ.
    Colossians 3:23–24

∽

Yet do this with gentleness and respect, keeping a clear conscience, so that when you are accused, those who disparage your good conduct in Christ will be put to shame.
    1 Peter 3:16

∽

*Search me, Lord God, and know my heart,
and if there is anything ungodly in me,
lead me in the way everlasting.*

JOY

Happiness can be fleeting, but joy is steadfast because it comes from the firm foundation of our intimacy with Christ.

∝

You reveal the path of life to me;
in your presence is abundant joy;
at your right hand are eternal pleasures.
        Psalm 16:11

∝

This is the day the LORD has made;
let us rejoice and be glad in it.
        Psalm 118:24

But the fruit of the Spirit is love, joy, peace, patience, kindness,
goodness, faithfulness, gentleness, and self-control. The law is not
against such things.
  Galatians 5:22–23

༄

"As the Father has loved me, I have also loved you. Remain in my love.
If you keep my commands you will remain in my love, just as I have kept
my Father's commands and remain in his love. I have told you these
things so that my joy may be in you and your joy may be complete."
  John 15:9–11

༄

Dear Jesus, thank You for the abundant joy
that comes from Your faithful presence.

JUSTICE

God's Word makes it clear how deeply He cares about the poor and the oppressed, and He calls us to act accordingly.

∽

Do not act unjustly when deciding a case. Do not be partial to the poor or give preference to the rich; judge your neighbor fairly.
    Leviticus 19:15

∽

Isn't this the fast I choose: To break the chains of wickedness, to untie the ropes of the yoke, to set the oppressed free, and to tear off every yoke? Is it not to share your bread with the hungry, to bring the poor and homeless into your house, to clothe the naked when you see him, and not to ignore your own flesh and blood?
    Isaiah 58:6–7

The LORD of Armies says this: "Make fair decisions. Show faithful love and compassion to one another. Do not oppress the widow or the fatherless, the resident alien or the poor, and do not plot evil in your hearts against one another."

Zechariah 7:9–10

৶

Don't be deceived: God is not mocked. For whatever a person sows he will also reap.

Galatians 6:7

৶

Pure and undefiled religion before God the Father is this: to look after orphans and widows in their distress and to keep oneself unstained from the world.

James 1:27

৶

Father God, please open my eyes and heart to the needs in my community and empower me to bring Your light to dark corners.

KINDNESS

In God's great kindness, He saved us through His beloved Son, and He now calls us to extend that same gentleness and compassion to others.

❧

He also raised us up with him and seated us with him in the heavens in Christ Jesus, so that in the coming ages he might display the immeasurable riches of his grace through his kindness to us in Christ Jesus.

Ephesians 2:6–7

❧

Let all bitterness, anger and wrath, shouting and slander be removed from you, along with all malice. And be kind and compassionate to one another, forgiving one another, just as God also forgave you in Christ.

Ephesians 4:31–32

Therefore, as God's chosen ones, holy and dearly loved, put on compassion, kindness, humility, gentleness, and patience.
    Colossians 3:12

∿

But when the kindness of God our Savior and his love for mankind appeared, he saved us—not by works of righteousness that we had done, but according to his mercy—through the washing of regeneration and renewal by the Holy Spirit.
    Titus 3:4–6

∿

Dear God, may Your Holy Spirit soften my speech and actions so that I display Your kindness to my spouse, children, colleagues, and neighbors today.

LEADERSHIP

A true leader isn't one who has climbed to the top of a hierarchy, but one who chooses to be a servant above all else.

❧

The slacker craves, yet has nothing,
but the diligent is fully satisfied.
Proverbs 13:4

❧

The one who is lazy in his work
is brother to a vandal.
Proverbs 18:9

Whatever you do, do it from the heart, as something done for the Lord and not for people, knowing that you will receive the reward of an inheritance from the Lord. You serve the Lord Christ.
    Colossians 3:23–24

∽

In fact, when we were with you, this is what we commanded you: "If anyone isn't willing to work, he should not eat."
    2 Thessalonians 3:10

∽

*Lord Jesus, You came not to be served
but to serve—please grant me Your Spirit
of servant leadership in my endeavors.*

LONELINESS

Modern life has left many of us feeling isolated—but thanks to God's faithful presence and our community of believers, we never have to be alone.

❦

"My presence will go with you, and I will give you rest."
Exodus 33:14

❦

The LORD is the one who will go before you. He will be with you; he will not leave you or abandon you. Do not be afraid or discouraged.
Deuteronomy 31:8

❦

God provides homes for those who are deserted.
He leads out the prisoners to prosperity,
but the rebellious live in a scorched land.
Psalm 68:6

He heals the brokenhearted
and bandages their wounds.
    Psalm 147:3

⁓

Blessed be the God and Father of our Lord Jesus Christ, the Father of
mercies and the God of all comfort. He comforts us in all our affliction,
so that we may be able to comfort those who are in any kind of affliction,
through the comfort we ourselves receive from God.
    2 Corinthians 1:3–4

⁓

Father of mercies, please comfort me in times of
loneliness so that I may be a comfort to others.

LOVE

Our highest calling is to love God with all of our heart, our soul, and our mind, and to love our neighbor as ourselves.

❧

"But I say to you who listen: Love your enemies, do what is good to those who hate you, bless those who curse you, pray for those who mistreat you."
    Luke 6:27–28

❧

Love is patient, love is kind. Love does not envy, is not boastful, is not arrogant, is not rude, is not self-seeking, is not irritable, and does not keep a record of wrongs.
    1 Corinthians 13:4–5

Above all, maintain constant love for one another, since love covers a multitude of sins.

1 Peter 4:8

≈

God's love was revealed among us in this way: God sent his one and only Son into the world so that we might live through him.

1 John 4:9

≈

And we have come to know and to believe the love that God has for us. God is love, and the one who remains in love remains in God, and God remains in him.

1 John 4:16

≈

Dear Jesus, instill in my heart the selfless concern and compassion for others that You demonstrated for us.

MARRIAGE

The covenantal union between a man and a woman is a symbol of our ultimate hope: the consummation of our union with the Lord Jesus.

℘

This is why a man leaves his father and mother and bonds with his wife, and they become one flesh.
    Genesis 2:24

℘

A man who finds a wife finds a good thing
and obtains favor from the LORD.
    Proverbs 18:22

℘

A house and wealth are inherited from fathers,
but a prudent wife is from the LORD.
    Proverbs 19:14

Wives, submit to your husbands as to the Lord, because the husband is the head of the wife as Christ is the head of the church. He is the Savior of the body. Now as the church submits to Christ, so also wives are to submit to their husbands in everything. Husbands, love your wives, just as Christ loved the church and gave himself for her to make her holy, cleansing her with the washing of water by the word. He did this to present the church to himself in splendor, without spot or wrinkle or anything like that, but holy and blameless. In the same way, husbands are to love their wives as their own bodies. He who loves his wife loves himself. For no one ever hates his own flesh but provides and cares for it, just as Christ does for the church, since we are members of his body. For this reason a man will leave his father and mother and be joined to his wife, and the two will become one flesh. This mystery is profound, but I am talking about Christ and the church. To sum up, each one of you is to love his wife as himself, and the wife is to respect her husband.

Ephesians 5:22–33

Marriage is to be honored by all and the marriage bed kept undefiled, because God will judge the sexually immoral and adulterers.

Hebrews 13:4

Heavenly Father, thank You for the gift of a spouse and may I love and support him just as You love and strengthen Your church.

MERCY

When the demands of life overwhelm you, remember that you can approach God's throne of grace with boldness.

✍

"Blessed are the merciful, for they will be shown mercy."
    Matthew 5:7

✍

"Go and learn what this means: I desire mercy and not sacrifice. For I didn't come to call the righteous, but sinners."
    Matthew 9:13

✍

Therefore, let us approach the throne of grace with boldness, so that we may receive mercy and find grace to help us in time of need.
    Hebrews 4:16

Speak and act as those who are to be judged by the law of freedom. For judgment is without mercy to the one who has not shown mercy. Mercy triumphs over judgment.

James 2:12–13

✧

Blessed be the God and Father of our Lord Jesus Christ. Because of his great mercy he has given us new birth into a living hope through the resurrection of Jesus Christ from the dead.

1 Peter 1:3

✧

Lord God, thank you for your mercy and lovingkindness in times of need.

MONEY

Money is an essential and valuable tool, but too much trust in it or too much desire for it can quickly lead us astray.

❧

"No one can serve two masters, since either he will hate one and love the other, or he will be devoted to one and despise the other. You cannot serve both God and money."
        Matthew 6:24

❧

Pay your obligations to everyone: taxes to those you owe taxes, tolls to those you owe tolls, respect to those you owe respect, and honor to those you owe honor.
        Romans 13:7

For the love of money is a root of all kinds of evil, and by craving it, some have wandered away from the faith and pierced themselves with many griefs.
    1 Timothy 6:10

❧

Instruct those who are rich in the present age not to be arrogant or to set their hope on the uncertainty of wealth, but on God, who richly provides us with all things to enjoy.
    1 Timothy 6:17

❧

Keep your life free from the love of money. Be satisfied with what you have, for he himself has said, "I will never leave you or abandon you."
    Hebrews 13:5

❧

Heavenly Father, who richly provides us with so much abundance, please keep my heart free from covetousness and the love of money.

MOTIVES

Rather than self-seeking or people-pleasing, we should endeavor to do all things through genuine love for God and others.

∽

But the LORD said to Samuel, "Do not look at his appearance or his stature because I have rejected him. Humans do not see what the LORD sees, for humans see what is visible, but the LORD sees the heart."
1 Samuel 16:7

∽

All a person's ways seem right to him,
but the LORD weighs hearts.
Proverbs 21:2

∽

Do nothing out of selfish ambition or conceit, but in humility consider others as more important than yourselves.
Philippians 2:3

For am I now trying to persuade people, or God? Or am I striving to please people? If I were still trying to please people, I would not be a servant of Christ.

Galatians 1:10

❧

Instead, just as we have been approved by God to be entrusted with the gospel, so we speak, not to please people, but rather God, who examines our hearts.

1 Thessalonians 2:4

❧

Lord, please weigh my heart and my reasons
for doing the things I do, and reveal to me
any motives that don't glorify You.

OBEDIENCE

Obedience to God means yielding our will to His, and His will is that we love Him and our neighbor as ourselves—on these two commandments depend all the law and the prophets.

❧

I have chosen the way of truth;
I have set your ordinances before me.
  Psalm 119:30

❧

"If you love me, you will keep my commands."
  John 14:15

❧

Peter and the apostles replied, "We must obey God rather than people."
  Acts 5:29

The one who keeps his commands remains in him, and he in him. And the way we know that he remains in us is from the Spirit he has given us.
    1 John 3:24

∽

For this is what love for God is: to keep his commands. And his commands are not a burden, because everyone who has been born of God conquers the world. This is the victory that has conquered the world: our faith.
    1 John 5:3–4

∽

Lord Jesus, may Your Spirit guide me in all my thoughts, words, and actions that I may be fully submitted to Your will.

PATIENCE

The liveliness of children or the demands of the workplace can rattle your nerves; but take care to avoid making wrong choices or damaging your relationships.

∽

The end of a matter is better than its beginning;
a patient spirit is better than a proud spirit.
    Ecclesiastes 7:8

∽

Now if we hope for what we do not see, we eagerly wait for it with patience.
    Romans 8:25

∽

My dear brothers and sisters, understand this: Everyone should be quick to listen, slow to speak, and slow to anger, for human anger does not accomplish God's righteousness.
    James 1:19–20

Therefore, brothers and sisters, be patient until the Lord's coming. See how the farmer waits for the precious fruit of the earth and is patient with it until it receives the early and the late rains. You also must be patient. Strengthen your hearts, because the Lord's coming is near.

James 5:7–8

∞

The Lord does not delay his promise, as some understand delay, but is patient with you, not wanting any to perish but all to come to repentance.

2 Peter 3:9

∞

Heavenly Father, You are patient and slow to anger—please help me be still and wait patiently for You.

PEACE

Rather than worry over what has happened in the past or what might happen in the future, be still with the Lord in the peace of the present moment.

✑

You will keep the mind that is dependent on you in perfect peace, for it is trusting in you.
    Isaiah 26:3

✑

"Peace I leave with you. My peace I give to you. I do not give to you as the world gives. Don't let your heart be troubled or fearful."
    John 14:27

For I am persuaded that neither death nor life, nor angels nor rulers, nor things present nor things to come, nor powers, nor height nor depth, nor any other created thing will be able to separate us from the love of God that is in Christ Jesus our Lord.

> Romans 8:38–39

∽

And the peace of God, which surpasses all understanding, will guard your hearts and minds in Christ Jesus. Finally brothers and sisters, whatever is true, whatever is honorable, whatever is just, whatever is pure, whatever is lovely, whatever is commendable—if there is any moral excellence and if there is anything praiseworthy—dwell on these things.

> Philippians 4:7–8

∽

*Lord Jesus, may Your perfect peace
guard my heart and mind as I trust in You.*

PRAYER

No matter how we come to the Lord, whether to present our requests or to sit silently in His presence, we can trust that He hears us.

✑

"Whenever you pray, you must not be like the hypocrites, because they love to pray standing in the synagogues and on the street corners to be seen by people. Truly I tell you, they have their reward. But when you pray, go into your private room, shut your door, and pray to your Father who is in secret. And your Father who sees in secret will reward you. When you pray, don't babble like the Gentiles, since they imagine they'll be heard for their many words. Don't be like them, because your Father knows the things you need before you ask him.

"Therefore, you should pray like this: Our Father in heaven, your name be honored as holy. Your kingdom come. Your will be done on earth as it is in heaven. Give us today our daily bread. And forgive us our debts, as we also have forgiven our debtors. And do not bring us into temptation, but deliver us from the evil one.

"For if you forgive others their offenses, your heavenly Father will forgive you as well. But if you don't forgive others, your Father will not forgive your offenses."

Matthew 6:5–15

"If you remain in me and my words remain in you, ask whatever you want and it will be done for you."
    John 15:7

℞

In the same way the Spirit also helps us in our weakness, because we do not know what to pray for as we should, but the Spirit himself intercedes for us with unspoken groanings.
    Romans 8:26

℞

Don't worry about anything, but in everything, through prayer and petition with thanksgiving, present your requests to God.
    Philippians 4:6

℞

Pray constantly.
    1 Thessalonians 5:17

℞

Lord Jesus, just as You taught Your followers how to pray, instill in me a deep desire to seek Your presence.

PRIDE

Though we may be blessed with wisdom, success, and happy relationships, we can avoid arrogance by remembering that all good things are ours by the grace of God.

∽

When arrogance comes, disgrace follows,
but with humility comes wisdom.
Proverbs 11:2

∽

Everyone with a proud heart is detestable to the LORD;
be assured, he will not go unpunished.
Proverbs 16:5

A person's pride will humble him,
but a humble spirit will gain honor.
       Proverbs 29:23

✍

Live in harmony with one another. Do not be proud; instead, associate
with the humble. Do not be wise in your own estimation.
       Romans 12:16

✍

For if anyone considers himself to be something when he is nothing, he
deceives himself.
       Galatians 6:3

✍

Father God, please forgive the ways I puff myself up
rather than humble myself under Your loving hand.

PURPOSE

Our deepest purpose is not in what we do but in who we are—people who love, honor, and praise God.

⚮

When all has been heard, the conclusion of the matter is this: fear God and keep his commands, because this is for all humanity.
    Ecclesiastes 12:13

⚮

"My Father is glorified by this: that you produce much fruit and prove to be my disciples."
    John 15:8

⚮

But I consider my life of no value to myself; my purpose is to finish my course and the ministry I received from the Lord Jesus, to testify to the gospel of God's grace.
    Acts 20:24

He has saved us and called us with a holy calling, not according to our works, but according to his own purpose and grace, which was given to us in Christ Jesus before time began.

2 Timothy 1:9

∽

Sing to him; sing praise to him; tell about all his wondrous works! Honor his holy name; let the hearts of those who seek the LORD rejoice.

1 Chronicles 16:9–10

∽

Lord Jesus, may each day offer me opportunities to live out my true purpose by loving and serving You and those around me.

RELATIONSHIPS

Loving relationships and friendships are gifts from God—we are built up and supported in community and in fellowship with other believers.

∽

Then the LORD God said, "It is not good for the man to be alone. I will make a helper corresponding to him."
    Genesis 2:18

∽

But if they do not have self-control, they should marry, since it is better to marry than to burn with desire.
    1 Corinthians 7:9

∽

Don't become partners with those who do not believe. For what partnership is there between righteousness and lawlessness? Or what fellowship does light have with darkness?
    2 Corinthians 6:14

Therefore encourage one another and build each other up as you are already doing.
    1 Thessalonians 5:11

∾

Above all, maintain constant love for one another, since love covers a multitude of sins.
    1 Peter 4:8

∾

*Heavenly Father, reveal to me ways
I can be a conduit of Your love toward
those in my community today.*

RIGHTEOUSNESS

God made the one who knew no sin to be sin for us, so that in Jesus we might become the very righteousness of God.

∽

How happy are those who uphold justice,
who practice righteousness at all times.
    Psalm 106:3

∽

"For I tell you, unless your righteousness surpasses that of the scribes
and Pharisees, you will never get into the kingdom of heaven."
    Matthew 5:20

∽

He made the one who did not know sin to be sin for us, so that in him we
might become the righteousness of God.
    2 Corinthians 5:21

But even if you should suffer for righteousness, you are blessed. Do not fear what they fear or be intimidated, but in your hearts regard Christ the Lord as holy, ready at any time to give a defense to anyone who asks you for a reason for the hope that is in you.

1 Peter 3:14–15

☙

Children, let no one deceive you. The one who does what is right is righteous, just as he is righteous.

1 John 3:7

☙

*Heavenly Father, may Your Spirit
guide me and empower me to glorify
You by doing what is right and just.*

SAVIOR

Christ Jesus is our Savior, the Source and Perfector of our faith, who for the joy set before Him endured the cross.

❧

He said, "They are indeed my people, children who will not be disloyal," and he became their Savior. In all their suffering, he suffered, and the angel of his presence saved them. He redeemed them because of his love and compassion; he lifted them up and carried them all the days of the past.

Isaiah 63:8–9

❧

My soul praises the greatness of the Lord, and my spirit rejoices in God my Savior, because he has looked with favor on the humble condition of his servant.

Luke 1:46–48

"This Jesus is the stone rejected by you builders, which has become the cornerstone. There is salvation in no one else, for there is no other name under heaven given to people by which we must be saved."

Acts 4:11–12

ꝏ

This is good, and it pleases God our Savior, who wants everyone to be saved and to come to the knowledge of the truth.

1 Timothy 2:3–4

ꝏ

And we have seen and we testify that the Father has sent his Son as the world's Savior.

1 John 4:14

ꝏ

Lord Jesus, I have been crucified with You—
may the life I now live be lived for You who
loved me and gave Yourself for me.

SECURITY

Our natural need for security won't be satisfied by alarm systems, personal strength, or a full bank account, but by trusting in the provision and protection of God.

∽

You will be confident, because there is hope.
You will look carefully about and lie down in safety.
    Job 11:18

∽

I always let the LORD guide me.
Because he is at my right hand,
I will not be shaken.
    Psalm 16:8

∽

And my God will supply all your needs according to his riches in glory in Christ Jesus.
    Philippians 4:19

He brought me up from a desolate pit,
out of the muddy clay,
and set my feet on a rock,
making my steps secure.
  Psalm 40:2

∽

The one who lives under the protection of the Most High
dwells in the shadow of the Almighty.
  Psalm 91:1

∽

Heavenly Father, thank You for Your promises to
supply all my needs and to make my steps secure.

SERVICE

Christ Jesus, the king of heaven, came not to be served but to serve others and set for us His example to follow.

∽

"And the King will answer them, 'Truly I tell you, whatever you did for one of the least of these brothers and sisters of mine, you did for me.'"
    Matthew 25:40

∽

"For even the Son of Man did not come to be served, but to serve, and to give his life as a ransom for many."
    Mark 10:45

I have been crucified with Christ, and I no longer live, but Christ lives in me. The life I now live in the body, I live by faith in the Son of God, who loved me and gave himself for me.

Galatians 2:20

❦

Therefore, my dear brothers and sisters, be steadfast, immovable, always excelling in the Lord's work, because you know that your labor in the Lord is not in vain.

1 Corinthians 15:58

❦

*Lord Jesus, please open my eyes to see
the myriad opportunities to serve my family,
colleagues, church, and community, and open
my heart to do so freely and with compassion.*

SPEECH

When we speak, the words we choose are only part of our response—we must also consider our motives and tone of voice.

∽

A gentle answer turns away anger,
but a harsh word stirs up wrath.
    Proverbs 15:1

∽

Let your speech always be gracious, seasoned with salt, so that you may know how you should answer each person.
    Colossians 4:6

∽

Bless those who persecute you; bless and do not curse.
    Romans 12:14

But no one can tame the tongue. It is a restless evil, full of deadly poison. With the tongue we bless our Lord and Father, and with it we curse people who are made in God's likeness. Blessing and cursing come out of the same mouth. My brothers and sisters, these things should not be this way.

James 3:8–10

∽

No foul language should come from your mouth, but only what is good for building up someone in need, so that it gives grace to those who hear.

Ephesians 4:29

∽

Holy Spirit, please fill my heart with the gracious love of God so that my speech is humble, gentle, and kind.

STRESS

Chronic stress is quickly becoming a national crisis that threatens our health—but God is our ever-present helper in times of trouble.

❧

Cast your burden on the LORD,
and he will sustain you;
he will never allow the righteous to be shaken.
    Psalm 55:22

❧

Commit your activities to the LORD,
and your plans will be established.
    Proverbs 16:3

❧

I am able to do all things through him who strengthens me.
    Philippians 4:13

For I am the LORD your God, who holds your right hand, who says to you, "Do not fear, I will help you."
    Isaiah 41:13

ॐ

"Come to me, all of you who are weary and burdened, and I will give you rest. Take up my yoke and learn from me, because I am lowly and humble in heart, and you will find rest for your souls. For my yoke is easy and my burden is light."
    Matthew 11:28–30

ॐ

Dear God, please fill me and strengthen me with Your Spirit when I feel overwhelmed, exhausted, and uncertain.

SUCCESS

Whether you succeed or fail at your endeavors, your true identity is your relationship with the Lord Jesus.

∽

Take delight in the LORD,
and he will give you your heart's desires.
      Psalm 37:4

∽

Commit your activities to the LORD,
and your plans will be established.
      Proverbs 16:3

"For what will it benefit someone if he gains the whole world yet loses his life? Or what will anyone give in exchange for his life? For the Son of Man is going to come with his angels in the glory of his Father, and then he will reward each according to what he has done."

    Matthew 16:26–27

ℝ

Humble yourselves before the Lord, and he will exalt you.

    James 4:10

ℝ

Lord Jesus, no matter how well I succeed in various aspects of my life, help me remember that my purpose is to be a shining beacon of Your light and love.

TEACHING

As wise and mature people of faith, we are called to teach our children the blessed Word and ways of the Lord.

❧

Until I come, give your attention to public reading, exhortation, and teaching.
	1 Timothy 4:13

❧

Preach the word; be ready in season and out of season; rebuke, correct, and encourage with great patience and teaching.
	2 Timothy 4:2

❧

Not many should become teachers, my brothers, because you know that we will receive a stricter judgment.
	James 3:1

In the same way, encourage the young men to be self-controlled in everything. Make yourself an example of good works with integrity and dignity in your teaching. Your message is to be sound beyond reproach, so that any opponent will be ashamed, because he doesn't have anything bad to say about us.

Titus 2:6–8

❧

Heavenly Father, as You have taught me through Your Word, may I be a source of godly instruction for my sons and daughters.

TEMPTATION

There are some temptations that are unavoidable, however God is faithful to provide an escape from what tempts you.

❧

"Stay awake and pray, so that you won't enter into temptation. The spirit is willing, but the flesh is weak."
    Matthew 26:41

❧

No temptation has come upon you except what is common to humanity. But God is faithful; he will not allow you to be tempted beyond what you are able, but with the temptation he will also provide a way out so that you may be able to bear it.
    1 Corinthians 10:13

For since he himself has suffered when he was tempted, he is able to help those who are tempted.
    Hebrews 2:18

✍

No one undergoing a trial should say, "I am being tempted by God," since God is not tempted by evil, and he himself doesn't tempt anyone. But each person is tempted when he is drawn away and enticed by his own evil desire. Then after desire has conceived, it gives birth to sin, and when sin is fully grown, it gives birth to death.
    James 1:13–15

✍

Therefore, submit to God. Resist the devil, and he will flee from you.
    James 4:7

✍

Lord God, my spirit is willing, but my flesh is weak—please help me to honor You in all of my choices.

THANKFULNESS

The more we practice gratitude and thanksgiving, the more abundance and goodness we recognize all around us.

❧

Give thanks to the LORD, for he is good;
his faithful love endures forever.
    Psalm 118:1

❧

For we know that the one who raised the Lord Jesus will also raise us
with Jesus and present us with you. Indeed, everything is for your benefit
so that, as grace extends through more and more people, it may cause
thanksgiving to increase to the glory of God.
    2 Corinthians 4:14–15

Let the word of Christ dwell richly among you, in all wisdom teaching and admonishing one another through psalms, hymns, and spiritual songs, singing to God with gratitude in your hearts.
    Colossians 3:16

❧

Rejoice always, pray constantly, give thanks in everything; for this is God's will for you in Christ Jesus.
    1 Thessalonians 5:16–18

❧

Every good and perfect gift is from above, coming down from the Father of lights, who does not change like shifting shadows.
    James 1:17

❧

Father of lights, I praise You and thank You for every good and perfect gift You have given.

TRUST

To trust the Lord is to believe what He has said about Himself: He is good, faithful, and sovereign.

⟡

The person who trusts in the LORD, whose confidence indeed is the LORD, is blessed. He will be like a tree planted by water: it sends its roots out toward a stream, it doesn't fear when heat comes, and its foliage remains green. It will not worry in a year of drought or cease producing fruit.

> *Jeremiah 17:7–8*

⟡

Wait for the LORD;
be strong, and let your heart be courageous.
Wait for the LORD.

> *Psalm 27:14*

I will be with you when you pass through the waters, and when you pass through the rivers, they will not overwhelm you. You will not be scorched when you walk through the fire, and the flame will not burn you.

   Isaiah 43:2

∽

And my God will supply all your needs according to his riches in glory in Christ Jesus.

   Philippians 4:19

∽

This is the confidence we have before him: If we ask anything according to his will, he hears us.

   1 John 5:14

∽

Dear God, thank You that all things work together for the good of those who love You and are called according to Your purpose.

VIOLENCE

Whether brute force or abusive language, Jesus stood against all forms of violence and oppression, submitting even to death on a cross.

♊

The LORD *examines the righteous,*
but he hates the wicked
and those who love violence.
    Psalm 11:5

♊

Don't envy a violent man
or choose any of his ways.
    Proverbs 3:31

"You have heard that it was said, An eye for an eye and a tooth for a tooth. But I tell you, don't resist an evildoer. On the contrary, if anyone slaps you on your right cheek, turn the other to him also."
    Matthew 5:38–39

∽

Then Jesus told him, "Put your sword back in its place because all who take up the sword will perish by the sword. Or do you think that I cannot call on my Father, and he will provide me here and now with more than twelve legions of angels?"
    Matthew 26:52–53

∽

Heavenly Father, help me realize that all the violence in the world originates in our human hearts, even mine. Cleanse us and make us people of peace.

WEALTH

God has provided richly for us with things to enjoy; therefore let us be gracious and generous toward those in need.

❧

Who do I have in heaven but you?
And I desire nothing on earth but you.
    Psalm 73:25

❧

"Don't store up for yourselves treasures on earth, where moth and rust destroy and where thieves break in and steal. But store up for yourselves treasures in heaven, where neither moth nor rust destroys, and where thieves don't break in and steal."
    Matthew 6:19–20

I know both how to make do with little, and I know how to make do with a lot. In any and all circumstances I have learned the secret of being content—whether well fed or hungry, whether in abundance or in need.

Philippians 4:12

∞

Instruct those who are rich in the present age not to be arrogant or to set their hope on the uncertainty of wealth, but on God, who richly provides us with all things to enjoy. Instruct them to do what is good, to be rich in good works, to be generous and willing to share, storing up treasure for themselves as a good foundation for the coming age, so that they may take hold of what is truly life.

1 Timothy 6:17–19

∞

*Lord Jesus, I praise You and thank You
that my richest gain is knowing You.*

WISDOM

Though we may have advanced degrees and years of experience, true wisdom comes from the Holy Spirit, who helps us discern what is true, good, and right.

✍

Teach us to number our days carefully
so that we may develop wisdom in our hearts.
    Psalm 90:12

✍

Do not be conformed to this age, but be transformed by the renewing
of your mind, so that you may discern what is the good, pleasing, and
perfect will of God.
    Romans 12:2

Yet to those who are called, both Jews and Greeks, Christ is the power of God and the wisdom of God, because God's foolishness is wiser than human wisdom, and God's weakness is stronger than human strength.
  1 Corinthians 1:24–25

∽

Now if any of you lacks wisdom, he should ask God—who gives to all generously and ungrudgingly—and it will be given to him.
  James 1:5

∽

Heavenly Father, who gives generously and freely, please fill me with Your wisdom for how to be a godly mother.

WORK

Our ability to work is a gift from God—we can create, serve, and produce for the good of the world around us, which glorifies the Creator.

❧

Commit your activities to the LORD,
and your plans will be established.
    Proverbs 16:3

❧

Do everything in love.
    1 Corinthians 16:14

❧

And God is able to make every grace overflow to you, so that in every
way, always having everything you need, you may excel in every good
work.
    2 Corinthians 9:8

Whatever you do, do it from the heart, as something done for the Lord and not for people, knowing that you will receive the reward of an inheritance from the Lord. You serve the Lord Christ.

Colossians 3:23–24

∽

Come now, you who say, "Today or tomorrow we will travel to such and such a city and spend a year there and do business and make a profit." Yet you do not know what tomorrow will bring—what your life will be! For you are like vapor that appears for a little while, then vanishes. Instead, you should say, "If the Lord wills, we will live and do this or that."

James 4:13–15

∽

Creator of all good things, grant me meaningful work and empower me to do everything as for You and not for people.

WORRY

Worry is false and useless fear—it's imagining and anticipating what might happen but probably won't.

∽

"Therefore I tell you: Don't worry about your life, what you will eat or what you will drink; or about your body, what you will wear. Isn't life more than food and the body more than clothing? Consider the birds of the sky: They don't sow or reap or gather into barns, yet your heavenly Father feeds them. Aren't you worth more than they? Can any of you add one moment to his life-span by worrying?"
  Matthew 6:25–27

∽

The Lord answered her, "Martha, Martha, you are worried and upset about many things, but one thing is necessary. Mary has made the right choice, and it will not be taken away from her."
  Luke 10:41–42

We know that all things work together for the good of those who love God, who are called according to his purpose.
   Romans 8:28

∽

Don't worry about anything, but in everything, through prayer and petition with thanksgiving, present your requests to God. And the peace of God, which surpasses all understanding, will guard your hearts and minds in Christ Jesus.
   Philippians 4:6–7

∽

Lord Jesus, I am often worried about many things—please grant me a heart like Mary, who rested at Your feet.

VERSE INDEX